I. INTRODUCTION

Scholars studying law and economics have identified four stages through which every legal dispute moves. The first stage involves an alleged injury which leads to the legal dispute. Second, the injured party decides whether to advance a claim. Once a claim is advanced, the plaintiff and defendant may negotiate a settlement of the complaint. If the negotiation fails, the dispute moves to litigation. By subdividing the legal process into these four stages, it is possible to study the interaction at any one stage in greater detail.

This paper models the third stage of this process, the negotiation between the Federal Trade Commission (FTC) and private parties interested in consummating horizontal mergers that may adversely affect competition. The FTC must decide whether to advance a claim against the merger and seek to block the transaction. If a claim is made, the merging parties may "fight" and force a resolution of the dispute through litigation by moving forward with the transaction. They may also "fold" and abandon the transaction or "settle" and enter into an agreement with the government to resolve the issues underlying the merger challenge. This decision to fight, fold or settle is somewhat more complicated than the standard settle or litigate question, because the prospective nature of the alleged competitive injury gives the defendant an opportunity to abandon the transaction before the injury occurs.

Section II of this paper sets the background for the analysis by discussing the institutional structure of the FTC, explaining the merger review process and then presenting an overview of a firm's options when faced with a decision by the FTC to block a merger. Section III surveys a number of FTC merger challenges, addresses the basic issues and defines the equations to be estimated. A multinomial model of a firm's fight, fold or settle decision is estimated in Section IV, followed by an interpretation of the results and an application of the model using both historical data and information from mergers proposed during fiscal 1992. We find that the most important determinant of firms' fight, fold or settle decision is the level of the competitive overlap associated with the relevant transaction. In particular, if the competitive overlap is a small percentage of the transaction, firms generally prefer to reach a negotiated settlement with the Commission. In such cases, the settlement decision appears largely unaffected by the underlying merits of the FTC's legal position. In other cases, the merits of the case do play an important role in the litigation decision. We also find that the potential efficiencies generated by the merger affect the firms' decision-making process, with firms more likely to fight and less likely to settle if the merger is expected to offer efficiencies.

II. ISSUES IN MERGER ENFORCEMENT

A. Background on the Federal Trade Commission

The FTC is a government agency charged, along with the Antitrust Division of the Department of Justice, with enforcing the antitrust laws. Much of the antitrust casework involves the evaluation of the competitive effects of proposed horizontal mergers.[1] To interdict a proposed merger, the FTC must obtain a preliminary injunction from a federal district court, with possible review from the relevant court of appeals. If the court declines to issue the injunction, the firms are free to merge.

Commission decisions are based on a majority vote of the five Commissioners, each appointed by the President and confirmed by the Senate for terms of up to seven years. In each matter, the Commissioners usually receive separate memoranda from both the staff and senior management of both the Bureau of Competition (BC) and Bureau of Economics (BE) to assist in their decision making

---

[1] FTC's merger enforcement also includes cases against consummated horizontal mergers, vertical transactions and conglomerate mergers when issues of potential competition exist. Such cases, however, are relatively rare and therefore do not present the opportunity for systematic analysis.

process. The parties also have an opportunity to present their positions to the Commissioners through submissions and meetings.[2]

B. Overview of the Merger Review Process

A legal dispute over a horizontal merger fits into the standard law and economics framework, although the prospective nature of the competitive injury requires a slight generalization of the model. Firms propose mergers based on the negotiated interests of the two parties. A small fraction of proposed mergers may threaten competition and present a risk of antitrust injury were they to be consummated. If the firms recognize the potential injury, they have the option to abandon the transaction. Parties, however, may have a difficult time *a priori* knowing how the FTC will react to their proposed transaction. (See Johnson and Parkman, 1991.) Little is generally known about the decision to advance a potentially anticompetitive merger, because of the secrecy of the merger negotiation process.

Given the firms choose to proceed, the Hart-Scott-Rodino (HSR) Act usually requires them to notify the government of the proposed transaction and observe a 30 day waiting period.[3] If the

---

[2] Enforcement decisions are based in part on the 1982 Merger Guidelines with its 1984 and 1992 revisions. The Guidelines use the Herfindahl index (the sum of the squares of the market share of all firms in the market) to define a safe harbor for mergers. If the post- merger Herfindahl is under 1000, the government will take no action. For post-merger Herfindahls between 1000-1800, the government may take action. If the Herfindahl is over 1800 and the change in the Herfindahl is over 100, the government will take a close look at the transaction. Experience with the Guidelines and recent court decisions show that evidence on the ease of entry or the competitive nature of the market may overcome the anticompetitive presumption associated with a high Herfindahl statistic. See Coate and McChesney (1992) and Coate (1992).

[3] Transactions are covered if a firm with assets or net sales of $100 million or more acquires an ownership interest in a firm with assets or net sales of at least $10 million or a firm with assets or net sales of $10 million of more acquires a firm with assets or net sales of at least $100 million (15 U.S.C. sec. 18A(a) (2)). Reporting requirements are triggered if as a result of the transaction, the acquiring firm would hold at least 15 percent of the stock in the target or more than $15 million of the target's voting securities (15 U.S.C. sec. 18A(a) (3)). See also Johnson and Parkman (1991). The government often learns of small uncovered transactions through the news media or informal channels. Then investigations occur, although the government lacks the formal waiting period requirements. Given the

(continued...)

government believes that the merger may raise competitive concerns, the government can issue a request for additional information and further delay the process. At the end of the investigation, the government chooses either to challenge the transaction or to close the investigation. The FTC's decision to prosecute has been modeled using data from the mid-1980s. Coate, Higgins and McChesney (1990) found that the FTC's decision to move against a merger depended heavily on case-specific facts, with the Commission more likely to challenge the transaction if the Herfindahl index was over the Merger Guidelines' threshold of 1800, barriers to entry existed, or if other factors made the market conducive to anticompetitive behavior.[4] Data generated by both BC and BE were statistically significant in explaining the FTC's decision.

If the government decides to challenge the transaction, the parties have three choices.[5] They can "fight" by moving forward and forcing the government obtain a court order to block the transaction. Alternatively, the parties can "fold" and abandon the transaction. Finally, the firms can "settle" by entering into a consent agreement with the government to spin off assets to eliminate the competitive concern. This paper attempts to provide a model for this "fight, fold or settle" decision by using data on FTC merger challenges from October 1983 to September 1991.

The final stage in the horizontal merger enforcement process is litigation. The government bears the burden of proof to establish the merger is likely to lessen competition substantially. Court

---

[3](...continued)
legal bills necessary to defend a small transaction can easily dwarf the efficiency benefits, firms in this situation almost always cooperate with the government's investigation.

[4] For a model of Canadian enforcement policy, see Khemani and Shapiro (forthcoming). They find that high market shares and barriers to entry make enforcement more likely, while import penetration makes enforcement less likely.

[5] The actual negotiation process may begin before the Commission has taken a formal vote to move against a merger. A vote, however, must be taken to issue a complaint against a transaction and accept a consent for public comment. While the Commission can reject consents after the public comment period, this rarely (if ever) occurs. Minor changes, however, may be made to account for technical problems overlooked in the initial negotiations.

decisions have divided the process into stages, with the government required to prove that the merger significantly raises concentration to a level that establishes a presumption that competition will be injured. The parties must then rebut the presumption that the merger is likely to lessen competition. A recent study of federal judicial merger decisions after the 1982 Merger Guidelines has found that the government must show a high Herfindahl statistic and barriers to entry in the relevant market to prevail in a merger case (Coate, 1992). Even in these cases, if the Herfindahl is not well over 1800, evidence on structural factors conducive to competition can rebut the presumption from a high Herfindahl. Thus, it appears that the merits of a case have a significant impact on the outcome of litigation.

Although in private litigation, these four stages would be interdependent (Perloff and Rubinfeld, 1988), we do not expect interdependence with the FTC as the plaintiff. The FTC would appear to base its enforcement decisions on a long run policy of preserving the competitive structure of the U. S. economy. We assume that the FTC has sufficient resources to enforce its merger policy, with the excess resources used for the nonmerger activity. Once a complaint is issued, we assume that the Commission is committed to litigating, unless the parties propose a settlement that resolves the government's concerns. In effect, we are assuming that parties cannot "cut a deal" with the Commission. We suggest two reasons for this assumption. First, as a repeat player in the merger game, the Commission must protect its reputation. (See a similar discussion along these lines in Perloff and Rubinfeld, 1988 at 156.) Second, as an administrative agency, the Commission can use its own administrative procedures to commit itself to a particular policy. (See McCubbins, Noll, and Weingast, 1987, and Fershtman and Judd, 1987.) Indeed, in practice, the Commission has the same attorneys who argued that a case be brought deal with the details of settlement. As Coate, Higgins, and McChesney (1990) point out, these attorneys are likely to be the strongest proponents of bringing the case. Thus, the respondents appear to face a finalized enforcement decision and can only

5

integrate the likelihood of success on the merits and the costs of litigation into their response. We focus on the issues affecting the respondents in our model.

C. Firms' Incentives When Faced With an FTC Challenge

Along the lines of the traditional settlement literature (for example, Landes 1971 at 66-67), when faced with an FTC decision to sue, we expect that firms will take the course of action with the highest expected value. In particular, the expected benefits of defeating the FTC (completing the merger) will be balanced against the costs of fighting the agency. For fighting to be the dominant strategy, the net benefits of litigation must exceed those of settling the case. If the net benefits to both fighting and settling are less than zero, the firm will abandon the transaction.

The benefits of fighting the FTC can be defined as the probability of defeating the FTC in court multiplied by the expected profits from consummating the transaction. We model the probability of prevailing in court as an inverse function of the merits of the FTC's case. In the next section, we present several measures of the merits of a case.

The benefit of victory has two possible components. The first is a positive function of the efficiencies associated with the transaction, as discussed below. The larger the efficiencies, the more likely that the firms will choose to fight the FTC.[6] The second possible benefit to the merging parties comes from the expected value of any anticompetitive actions that the merger makes possible. We will use the same merits variables as we use for the probability of defeating the FTC in court. Note, however, that the merits of the case may have an ambiguous effect on a firm's decision to fight

---

[6] It is unlikely that efficiencies were recognized as an antitrust defense during our period of study. Even if efficiencies were thought to have a significant impact on the outcome of the case, the 1984 Guidelines stated that the defense should be based on "clear and convincing" evidence. Appeals Court Judge and former Assistant Attorney General for Antitrust Ginsburg (1991 at 97) has recently called reaching this standard "well-nigh impossible." Further, even if defendants can meet this level of proof, only efficiencies in the relevant anticompetitive market may count. See also FTC v. University Health, Inc., 938 F.2d 1206 (11th Cir. 1991) and Joskow (1991 at 66).

the FTC, because an increase in the merits of the case reduces the likelihood of victory in the litigation, while possibly increasing the returns to the merger.

Fighting the FTC entails costs. The most obvious costs are the legal fees involved in defending the merger in a preliminary injunction hearing. Further costs arise because the FTC has a policy of always following a preliminary injunction case with a complaint to its own administrative law system. (See Lopatka and Mongoven, 1992.) These proceedings, with hearings before an administrative law judge, an appeal to the FTC sitting as a court, and then (if the FTC rules for its own staff and against the merger) an appeal to a federal circuit court, can take years. We suggest, however, that these costs can be viewed as relatively constant across firms.[7]

Litigation against the FTC may also force the firm to incur opportunity costs, because the firm forgoes a settlement that would bring the process to a quick resolution. The typical textbook example of an anticompetitive merger involves two firms competing to sell a product in a highly concentrated market, a scenario that leaves little room for settlement. In the modern world of conglomerate firms, however, a merger may involve both competitive overlaps and wide areas where the firms are not related at all. In such acquisitions, the firms would desire to consummate the noncontested portion of the merger quickly and deal with the contested portion later.

There is, however, no simple legal mechanism currently available to allow a partial acquisition to occur. The FTC has the ability to hold up the entire acquisition while seeking a preliminary injunction to block a relatively small aspect of the deal. (See Kolasky, Proger, and Englert, 1985 at 52.) In such situations, a firm may have a strong incentive to reach a settlement with the Commission, spin off the contested assets, and allow the remainder of the transaction to proceed. Thus, the firms would desire to settle with the Commission on the Commission's terms,

---

[7] While one could argue that some legal expenses are marginal costs and could be adjusted in response to the potential benefits of winning, many costs associated with an administrative trial are fixed and thus large transactions are more likely to end in litigation.

even if the merits of the Commission's case are weak. (See a similar discussion along these lines in Posner, 1972 at 381.) Here we seek to test this hypothesis by focusing on the "overlap" or share of the transaction subject to the competitive concerns. We therefore suggest that the FTC may have powers more similar to a regulatory commission than a prosecutor subject to judicial review under a "preponderance of the evidence" standard. Under this hypothesis, the Commission may be able to stop many more mergers than the case law would imply.

This desire to settle, however, may also be affected by the available efficiencies. A transaction is consummated when the acquiring firm believes that it can profitably operate the acquired assets, given the sales price. If a settlement would require the acquiring firm to divest a large portion of the assets, the efficiencies may be lost and the transaction may no longer be viable. Thus, the deal may collapse if a settlement eliminates significant efficiencies.

Any model of the "fight, fold or settle" process must take into account the interrelationships among the choices. A firm may evaluate the costs and benefits of both fighting and settling, but then must choose the alternative that maximizes its expected returns. Thus, the model must allow for the simultaneous nature of the decisions. Within this model, we expect firms to be more likely to litigate when the merits of a case are weak, while a conglomerate transaction will make settlement more likely. Finally, firms perceiving that the potential merger will create efficiencies will be more likely to litigate and less inclined to settle.

III. DATA AND ECONOMETRIC TECHNIQUES

A. Review of the Data

To construct the data set, we reviewed all 78 of the Commission's attempts to enjoin horizontal transactions between fiscal years 1984 to 1991. We include those cases in which the parties have offered a settlement, but exclude the transactions that are abandoned before Commission action.[8] Cases were then deleted from the sample when the merger involved a partial stock acquisition (1 case), when the Commission did not have sufficient notice to complete a full investigation before moving to enjoin the merger in court (2 cases) or when the transaction was characterized as a joint venture (3 cases). This left a total of 72 cases in which the Commission voted for a complaint against a prospective merger. The parties to the transaction then made one of three choices, to litigate (13 cases or 18 percent), to abandon the transaction (30 cases or 41 percent) or to enter into a settlement with the Commission (29 cases or 40 percent).

To evaluate the relative merits of the particular challenged mergers, we reviewed both BC and BE the staff memoranda. Each memo contained an analysis of the basic facts of the case, such as the Herfindahl index, ease of entry and competitive effects (e.g. ability to exploit market power). The BE data showed much more variance than the BC data. Generally, BC memos noted the Herfindahl was high, barriers to entry were present and anticompetitive behavior was possible, especially in the mid-to-late 1980's, when the BC staff had become very familiar with writing memos consistent with the Guidelines methodology.[9]

The BE memos were significantly different, with some case evaluations having relatively low Herfindahls, other case discussions noting no barriers to entry and still other case reviews finding no theory of anticompetitive effects. We believe that the BE data represent the best available proxy for the competitive potential of the merger, because such analysis falls between that of the parties (all

---

[8] By checking the records on second requests issued, Commission enforcement actions and agency files we found very few transactions were abandoned after the staff completed their analysis, but before the Commission decision. In a few cases, withdrawn deals were refiled latter and the Commission moved to enjoin the transaction. Thus, almost all of the mergers withdrawn before a Commission vote were abandoned because either (1) the deal collapsed or (2) the cost of H-S-R compliance was too high.

[9] This observation does not imply that the BC analyses are biased. The sample of 72 cases were all recommended by BC staff, so one may expect BC staff would believe that they are all meritorious cases. Numerous other investigations were closed, with BC analysis showing low Herfindahls, low barriers or no anticompetitive story. For a further discussion, see Coate, Higgins, and McChesney (1990) and Coate and McChesney (1992).

proposed mergers are procompetitive) and the BC staff (all challenged mergers are anticompetitive). In the few cases involving multiple overlaps, the data from the most anticompetitive overlap is recorded.

A number of the memoranda also contained limited information on merger-related efficiencies. Although these analyses did not always generate a clear recommendation as to the relevance or the level of efficiencies, we believe it is reasonable to measure the strength of the efficiency concerns by the number of pages dedicated to dealing with the efficiency question in both the BE and BC analyses.[10] In effect, the strength of the parties' efficiency defense is measured by the number of pages in the staff memos needed to explain these issues to the Commission. The discussions in the staff memos are in very large part a response to the parties' efficiency claims. We note that the FTC (and Department of Justice) policy of requiring evidence to support efficiency claims gives parties incentives to make presentations when they have such evidence and not to make such presentations when they do not.

The memos presented a wealth of background data such as the sales of the acquiring firm, the acquired entity and the parent company, the price of the transaction, and the magnitude of the competitive overlap. All of the sales and price figures were converted into real terms with annual (1982-based) GNP deflators. The overlap figure (OVERLAP) was estimated by the percentage of the deal subject to the competitive concerns, usually by dividing the sales in the market(s) under investigation by the total sales of the target entity.[11] When sales data were not available, other proxies such as the ratio of the number of stores in the geographic market(s) of concern to the total

---

[10] For the construction of a similar variable, see Coate and McChesney (1992). We found no evidence that staff or management at the agency engages in explicit tradeoffs of anticompetitive and efficiency effects of mergers, contrary to the analysis of Comanor and White (1992).

[11] All the overlaps subject to merger challenge are counted in the overlap variable, because the Commission tends to obtain full settlements. It would make little sense for a party to settle one overlap, just to go through a trial on the merits on other overlaps.

number of stores sold were used. Finally, the memos contained the date they were forwarded to the Commission, which is used to define the general time of Commission action. By computing the time in months from a base at January 1984 (the date of the first case in the sample), it is possible to test for changes in the probabilities of the various outcomes over the sample time period. Finally, other Commission records were reviewed to determine the outcome of each transaction.

B. An Initial Look at the Data

A firm's fight, fold or settle decision is likely to be based on a number of case-specific variables. These variables may include those mentioned in Section II, the merits of the case, efficiencies, the size of the transaction and extent of the competitive overlap, as well as other factors such as the size of the acquiring firm, time and foreign ownership. Some insight into how the relevant variables affect the decision making process can be obtained by examining how the variables are related to the firm's ultimate decision.

Table 1 compares the extent of the overlap to the final fight, fold or settle decision. It clearly shows that the probability of settlement is correlated with the relative size of the overlap. Overlaps of ten percent or less almost always (94 percent in the sample) result in settlements, while overlaps of up to 30 percent usually (77 percent) end in settlements. On the other hand, large overlaps of over 50 percent almost always (94 percent) lead to either litigation or the abandonment of the deal. Firms appear most willing to fight when the overlap involves almost the entire transaction and are relatively more likely to abandon the deal when the area of concern involves a significant fraction of the transaction. These results are consistent with the hypothesis that firms will not delay a transaction to litigate a small dispute.

Table 1
Percentage of Fight, Fold, and Settle by Overlap

OVERLAP	Total	Fight	Fold	Settle
91 - 100	18	8 (44.4%)	9 (50.0%)	1 (5.6%)
81 - 90	3	1 (33.3%)	2 (66.7%)	0 (0.0%)
71 - 80	2	0 (0.0%)	2 (100.0%)	0 (0.0%)
61 - 70	4	1 (25.0%)	3 (75.0%)	0 (0.0%)
51 - 60	5	1 (20.0%)	3 (60.0%)	1 (20.0%)
41 - 50	5	1 (20.0%)	3 (60.0%)	1 (20.0%)
31 - 40	4	0 (0.0%)	2 (50.0%)	2 (50.0%)
21 - 30	3	1 (33.3%)	1 (33.3%)	1 (33.3%)
11 - 20	11	0 (0.0%)	4 (36.4%)	7 (63.6%)
1 - 10	17	0 (0.0%)	1 (5.9%)	16 (94.1%)
Total	72	13 (18.1%)	30 (41.7%)	29 (40.3%)

Table 2 presents the average values for a number of variables for the given fight, fold or settle outcomes. The average OVERLAP was 82.7 percent in the litigated cases, 62.7 percent in the abandoned cases and only 17.3 percent in the settled cases. Likewise, the mean of the page-based efficiency variable is 22.5 pages for the litigated cases, but only 11.5 for the abandoned cases and 5.3 for the settled cases. Both the differences in the average overlap and efficiencies are statistically significant. The Bureau of Economic's estimate of the Herfindahl (HERF) and the estimate of the change in the Herfindahl (CHERF) are both lower when the case goes to litigation than otherwise. This result does not apply, however, to the barrier to entry and competitive effects variables. BE staff found barriers in approximately 85 percent of the mergers that ended in either litigation or abandonment. Moreover, the BE staff appears more likely to have put forward an explanation of anticompetitive effects (labelled "collusion" in Table 2, but also including hypothesized dominant firm behavior) for those mergers that ended in litigation. None of these differences, however, are statistically significant.

Table 2
Variables Means by Fight, Fold and Settle Status
(Standard Deviations In Parentheses)

Variable	Fight N=13	Fold N=30	Settle N=29	Overall N=72
OVERLAP[1,2,3]	82.69 (26.54)	62.73 (32.32)	17.34 (20.65)	48.06 (37.55)
Efficiencies[1,2,3]	22.50 (19.2)	11.53 (11.97)	5.345 (6.744)	11.02 (13.27)
HERF	3647 (1974)	3960 (2120)	4664 (3170)	4187 (2574)
CHERF	1083 (1017)	1209 (1073)	1443 (1695)	1277 (1341)
Barriers	.8462 (.376)	.8667 (.346)	.6897 (.471)	.7917 (0.409)
Collusion	.7692 (.438)	.7000 (.466)	.6207 (.494)	.6806 (0.470)
HERFB	2985 (2312)	3766 (2396)	3526 (3861)	3529 (3034)
HERFC	2985 (2312)	3633 (2546)	3483 (3894)	3456 (3096)
HERFBC	2548 (2569)	3213 (2746)	3268 (3860)	3115 (3249)
VALUE[2,3]	134.1 (203.2)	88.95 (117.7)	1969 (4384)	854.5 (2906)
SALES[2]	2598 (4123)	5266 (7743)	7592 (1184)	5721 (8944)
Foreign[1]	0 (0)	.1333 (.346)	.06897 (.258)	.08333 (.278)
OVERLAPA[2,3]	94.0 (21.63)	89.30 (28.2)	22.93 (29.31)	64.50 (43.13)
TIME	44.23 (29.3)	55.63 (23.15)	51.62 (27.83)	51.96 (26.19)

Log Formulations of Key Variables

Efficiencies[1,2,3]	2.780 (0.95)	2.125 (0.944)	1.443 (0.894)	1.969 (1.037)
VALUE[2,3]	3.934 (1.41)	3.876 (1.1023)	6.061 (1.726)	4.766 (1.775)
SALES[1,2]	6.354 (2.21)	7.519 (1.698)	8.079 (1.387)	7.534 (1.77)
HERFB	6.832 (3.054)	7.182 (2.892)	5.699 (3.943)	6.521 (3.406)
Efficiencies-2[1,2,3]	.1051 (.0884)	.06283 (.0610)	.03121 (.0374)	.05784 (.0642)

[1] indicates that the mean of the variable for fight outcomes is statistically different from the mean for fold outcomes at the 10 percent level.

[2] indicates that the mean of the variable for fight outcomes is statistically different from the mean for settle outcomes at the 10 percent level.

[3] indicates that the mean of the variable for fold outcomes is statistically different from the mean for settle outcomes at the 10 percent level.

Bold highlighting of the superscripted numbers indicates that the relevant means are different at the five percent level. Also, all t-tests allow for differences in the variances. Assuming equal variances would increase the number of significant differences.

An overall measure of the economic merits of the case would integrate the various structural variables into one summary index.[12] For example, an index variable (HERFB) can be defined as the product of the Herfindahl variable and the entry barrier dummy variable. If barriers were thought to

---

[12] Although a model could consider both the level and the change in the Herfindahl, the high correlation (0.91) between these two variables makes this approach difficult. Caution should be used when applying the model to a fact situation of a merger that results in either a small change in the Herfindahl in a very concentrated market or a large change in the Herfindahl in a moderately concentrated market.

be present, the index would take on the value of the Herfindahl and proxy the likelihood of a competitive problem. On the other hand, if barriers were considered low, the index would be zero indicating that anticompetitive effects were unlikely. A more sophisticated index (HERFC) integrates the projected competitive effects variable into the analysis only for relatively low levels of concentration. In particular, if the Herfindahl was under 2400 (and barriers present), one would require some evidence that collusion was likely before using the Herfindahl index as the proxy for the anticompetitive effect.[13] On the other hand, if the Herfindahl index exceeded 2400, one could simply use the Herfindahl to proxy the anticompetitive effect if barriers were high. Thus, the aggregate variable would be the Herfindahl if either the Herfindahl was over 2400 with barriers present or the Herfindahl was under 2400 but both barriers were present and a BE presentation of a collusion story existed for how the merger would reduce competition. Another structural index (HERFBC) indicates a possible competitive problem when barriers were present and a collusive or dominant firm story could be told. This variable would be defined by interacting the Herfindahl, the barrier to entry dummy and the collusion dummy.

Also of interest is the price of the transaction (VALUE). Very large deals tend to settle, with the average settlement being a billion dollar transaction, compared to an average of a little over 100 million dollars for litigated cases and a little under 100 million dollars for abandoned transactions. Likewise, the average revenue (SALES) of the firm involved in a settlement tends to be larger than the average firm that folds or fights, although the difference is not significant. A foreign firm dummy variable (Foreign) was defined as one if the acquiring firm was based overseas and zero if the acquiring firm was based in the U. S., regardless of the actual ownership of the company's stock.

---

[13] In a study of court decisions, it appeared possible to reject the presumption of an anticompetitive effect if the Herfindahl fell around 2400. However, if the Herfindahl exceeded 3000, it would be very unlikely for the government to fail on the merits after establishing entry impediments. See Coate (1992).

This approach assumes that the domestic subsidiaries of foreign companies negotiate with the FTC in the same way as domestic corporations.

The OVERLAPA variable allows a test of the robustness of the overlap relationship. OVERLAPA is derived from OVERLAP, with the value changed to 100 percent when a divestiture could require selling the entire business. For example, a firm composed of multi-product plants (with at least one product subject to a competitive concern) will be assigned a value of 100 percent, instead of a ratio based on the sales linked to the competitive concern, because a divestiture could require selling all the plants.[14] Sophisticated divestitures, however, such as selling equipment or technology, may be possible[15] so the adjusted overlap variable may not be necessary. The variable, however, does allow for a test of the robustness of the result. The final variable represents the average monthly time associated with each type of outcome. Generally, these results support our theories with small overlaps and large transactions more likely to settle and weak structural cases or clear efficiencies more likely to litigate. Because the variables may be interrelated, however, a more sophisticated analysis is needed to fully evaluate the fight, fold or settle decision.

Table 2 also presents the means for the natural logarithms of a number of key variables.[16] The variable names match those used in the first part of the table, with the exception of Efficiencies-2 which is defined by the ratio of the pages in the BC and BE memos on efficiencies to the total

---

[14] The construction of the OverlapA variable is not exogenous, because the classification of the transactions required judgement that occurred after the fight, fold or settle decision was made. The Overlap variable was based on data in the memos written before the outcome of the transaction was known.

[15] See, for example, "In the Matter of RWE/Vista," 56 Federal Register 28896 (June 25, 1992) where the Commission required a technology license to solve a horizontal overlap problem.

[16] If part of the data would take on the value zero, a one is added to the entire series to ensure the log function is defined for the entire data set. A small faction of one could also be used instead of one without changing the later results.

number of pages in the memos. The logarithmic formulations will be used in the later statistical analysis to allow the variables to have a nonlinear effect.

C. Econometric Techniques

The basic econometric problem involves the estimation of a model in which the decision maker chooses one of three mutually exclusive options: fight, fold or settle. The three choices complicate the estimation in comparison to the standard technique for a binary dependent variable. Since one of the three courses of action always occurred, we are left with two interdependent equations. We choose to focus on a fight equation and a settle equation and use a conditional logit procedure to estimate the ratio of the odds of fighting over folding and the ratio of the odds of settling over folding are estimated in one model.

The independent variables, discussed above, form the basis of the model. The competitive overlap, defined as the share of the transaction subject to competitive concerns, is a crucial variable. Large overlaps will make the firm more likely to litigate, because efficiencies are likely to be larger than the costs of litigation when the overlap involves almost the entire transaction. As the overlap shrinks, firms can be expected to be much more willing to settle, because a settlement avoids delaying the bulk of the transaction. Hence, we expect a positive sign on the coefficient for OVERLAP in the fight equation and a negative sign in the settle equation.

A pure efficiency variable, measured as the log of the number of pages in the staff analyses, would also be expected to positively affect firms' willingness to litigate. Given litigation is the only way that a firm could capture merger-specific cost savings, the magnitude of these savings should affect the firm's decision. Settlements, which almost always require divestitures and the loss of some efficiencies, are likely to be negatively related to the magnitude of the efficiencies if too much of the

17

value of the efficiencies were capitalized in the price of the transaction.[17] Thus, a positive sign is expected on the efficiency variable in the fight equation, while a negative effect could be found in the settle equation.

The merits variable appears best measured as the interaction of the Herfindahl variable and the barriers-to-entry variable using BE data, although other proxies for the merits will be considered. This variable was left in nominal form to allow competitive concerns to increase relatively linearly with the Herfindahl. It is also possible to consider a competitive effects theory in which evidence on barriers is sufficient to conclude the merger is likely to substantially lessen competition if the Herfindahl is over 2400, but data on ease of collusion is also required if the Herfindahl is between 1000 and 2400. Other measures include the simple Herfindahl and a variable that interacts the Herfindahl, the barrier to entry variable and the anticompetitive theory dummy variable. Assuming the reduction in the likelihood of success in court associated with a higher merits variable outweighed the additional anticompetitive gain when the firm prevailed, one would expect the structure index to find a negative effect on the fight equation. The expected effect in the settlement equation is ambiguous and depends on whether firms settle due to the merits of their case (positive effect expected) or due to a desire to proceed with the remainder of the transaction (no effect expected).

The value of the transaction is also included, because large deals may be more likely to be able to cover transactions costs of either litigation or settlements than small deals. It appears that a conditional formulation is appropriate for this variable. If the litigation strategy is chosen, the firm can expect to consummate the entire deal and the value of the transaction is the appropriate magnitude variable. On the other hand, if the firm settles, it really only consummates part of the transaction.

---

[17] A significant negative effect would also be found if staff knew which cases were likely to settle and shortened the discussion on efficiencies. Staff, however, would be expected to shorten the entire memo, so an efficiency variable based on share of the memo attributed to efficiencies would minimize this problem.

Thus, the appropriate value variable can be estimated by multiplying the share of the deal retained (1 - OVERLAP) by the value of the deal. In effect, the acquiring firm only obtains a fraction of the transaction and the larger this fraction, the more likely that it will cover the transaction costs of the settlement. In both situations, the variables were put in logarithmic form to represent the expected nonlinear nature of the relationship. This generalization of the multinomial logit technique is straightforward to implement, but the coefficient for the VALUE variable is restricted to be the same for both the fight and settle equations. We expect it will take on a positive sign, indicating that large transactions are more likely to end in litigation and deals where the acquiring firm retains a large value are more likely to end in settlements.

The size of the acquiring firm (SALES) was included to allow for a firms' decision to be influenced by its general policy on governmental relations. Theory does not predict which sign this variable will take. Large firms may expect many more interactions with government regulators than small firms. Thus, their behavior in any one interaction should take into account potential effects on later interactions. For example, a large firm could be more likely to litigate to establish a reputation for toughness along the lines of Milgrom and Roberts (1982). On the other hand, the large firm could be less likely to litigate to avoid causing problems with future government encounters.

Finally, a time variable (TIME) is included to test if the incentives of firms changed over the Reagan/Bush era. It is difficult to do more than speculate about the effects of trends in how firms respond to their regulators. For example, firms could be more willing to settle if the FTC relaxed the standards for a negotiated settlement, while the changes in capital markets could make transactions less profitable and reduce the likelihood of litigation.

IV. ESTIMATION OF THE MODEL

A. Presentation of the Results

The multinomial logit model is defined by two equations: one for the odds of the fight versus fold variable and the other for the odds of the settle versus fold variable. The value variable is set equal to the value of the firm being acquired, given the choice made by the parties. Thus, if the parties accept a divestiture settlement, VALUE will equal the value of the target company minus the value of the assets to be divested. This requires us to use McFadden's conditional multinomial logit model, which sets the coefficient on VALUE equal in both the fight and the settle equations. (See Maddala, 1986 at 59-61.) The equations then allow for the calculation of the probability of each of the three action given the values for the independent variables. Let B_1 equal the regression coefficients for the fight equation, B_2 the regression coefficients for the settle equation, z the coefficient for value in both equations, y_{ij} the level of VALUE in the i'th observation for the j'th outcome and X_i the attributes of the i'th observation. Let $A = B_1'X_i + zy_{i1}$ and $B = B_2'X_i + zy_{i2}$. Using the conditional logit model the probability of fighting equals

$$(1) \qquad P_1 = e^A/(1 + e^A + e^B)$$

while the probability of settling equals

$$(2) \quad P_2 = e^B/(1 + e^A + e^B),$$

implying that the probability of folding equals

$$(3) \quad P_3 = 1 - P_1 - P_2.$$

Table 3 presents the results of the basic model and three additional specifications with different merits variables. The column headings define the merits' variables used as the STRUCTURE variable. All other variables are the same for each run of the model. All of the models pass the Chi-square test at the 1% level.

The significance statistics show the Herfindahl-barrier (HERFB) variable and the Herfindahl-barrier/collusion (HERFC) variable[18] appear to affect the likelihood of litigation, while the simple Herfindahl (HERF) variable and the complex Herfindahl-barrier-competitive effects (HERFBC) variable do not have significant coefficients. Both HERFB and HERFC generate significant negative effects on the likelihood of a litigation. Thus, the statistical analysis gives some support to the hypothesis that the opportunity to succeed on the merits outweighs the incentive to capture anticompetitive profits related to a high structural index in litigation decisions.

The other control variables all have similar effects in the four equations. A higher overlap variable increases the odds on litigation vs. folding and reduces the relative likelihood of settling. Both effects are statistically significant. The efficiency variable also has the expected and statistically significant effects. The time variable has no significant impact on the odds of litigation and only a very weak effect on the odds of settlement.[19] Finally, the value of the transaction has a positive impact on the ratio of probability of litigation to folding and the value of the transaction (after adjustment for divestiture) also serves to increase the probability of a settlement.[20]

Table 4 presents a more general robustness check on the results. The first column presents the basic model with the interaction Herfindahl-barrier variable (HERFB) in log form to match the other independent variables. This specification does not change the significance of any of the results.

---

[18] Similar results are generated if the critical concentration level of 2,400 is adjusted up or down.

[19] A dummy variable equal to zero for the Reagan administration and one for the Bush administration is not significant in explaining the settlement or litigation decision.

[20] The model tests for the independence of irrelevant alternatives by estimating the parameters without either the fight or settle cases along the lines of Hausman and McFadden (1984). In either situation, the coefficient estimates were almost identical, with Hausman statistics of 0.80 and 12.8 respectively. Neither coefficient is significant, indicating that the hypothesis of equal coefficients cannot be rejected.

Table 3
Multinomial Logit Model with Various Merits Variables

	HERFB	HERFC	HERFBC	HERF
VALUE	.7664**	.7796**	.6353**	.6719**
	(2.37)	(2.42)	(2.18)	(2.26)

Fight Equation

	HERFB	HERFC	HERFBC	HERF
OVERLAP	.03977**	.03948**	.03915**	.03989**
	(2.19)	(2.22)	(2.18)	(2.25)
Efficiencies	1.626**	1.622**	1.447**	1.442**
	(2.40)	(2.41)	(2.18)	(2.20)
STRUCTURE	-.0004086*	-.0003963*	-.0001754	-.0001619
	(-1.74)	(-1.68)	(1.02)	(-0.73)
Time	-.01925	-.01935	-.01510	-.01327
	(-.89)	(-.89)	(-.73)	(-.66)
Sales	-1.032**	-1.047**	-.7769**	-.7320**
	(-2.45)	(-2.47)	(-2.26)	(-2.19)
Constant	-1.174	-1.148	-3.060	-3.520
	(-.28)	(-.28)	(-.77)	(-.86)

Settle Equation

	HERFB	HERFC	HERFBC	HERF
OVERLAP	-.04930**	-.04904**	-.05195**	-.04964**
	(-2.06)	(-2.06)	(-2.20)	(-2.10)
Efficiencies	-1.102**	-1.109**	-1.087**	-1.107**
	(-2.19)	(-2.20)	(-2.19)	(-2.20)
STRUCTURE	.00000480	.00003537	.00002269	.0001884
	(.03)	(.23)	(.16)	(.98)
Time	.03149	.03100	.02836	.02759
	(1.47)	(1.45)	(1.35)	(1.29)
Sales	.1936	.2116	.2478	.3466
	(.51)	(.56)	(.69)	(.93)
Constant	-2.792	-3.074	-2.474	-4.127
	(-.78)	(-.86)	(-.72)	(-1.08)
Pseudo R-square	0.549	0.547	0.532	0.535
Chi-square	82.30	82.06	79.84	80.94

T-statistics in parentheses, * indicates significance at the 10 percent level and ** indicates a five percent level

Robustness Analysis for Multinomial Logit Model

	Log(HERFB)	OVERLAPA	ADJUSTED EFFICIENCIES	FOREIGN
VALUE	.7226**	1.389**	.7670**	.6494**
	(2.16)	(3.17)	(2.48)	(2.02)
Fight Equation				
OVERLAP	.03815**	2.583*	.03360**	.03845**
	(2.07)	(1.76)	(2.08)	(2.03)
Efficiencies	1.710**	1.386**	14.76**	1.961**
	(2.37)	(2.46)	(2.21)	(2.41)
HERFB	-.2852	-.0006127**	-.0003625*	-.0005150**
	(-1.61)	(-2.33)	(-1.68)	(-2.05)
Time	-.02638	-.02472	-.03056	-.003240
	(-1.14)	(-1.18)	(-1.42)	(-.13)
Sales	-.9382**	-1.548**	-.9894**	-1.131**
	(-2.26)	(-3.23)	(-2.51)	(-2.49)
Constant	-.8581	1.998	2.126	-.9302
	(-.19)	(.54)	(.59)	(-.22)
Foreign	--	--	--	-21.36
				(-.001)
Settle Equation				
OVERLAP	-.0508**	-3.962**	-.04822**	-.05414**
	(-1.99)	(-3.40)	(-2.16)	(-2.20)
Efficiencies	-1.008**	-.9084*	-13.89	-1.027**
	(-2.04)	(-1.74)	(-1.51)	(-1.98)
HERFB	-.2451	-.000009269	-.000007850	-.00002786
	(-1.34)	(-.06)	(-.05)	(-.18)
Time	.03432	.03820	.03525*	.03472
	(1.59)	(1.58)	(1.79)	(1.51)
Sales	.1789	.03711	.09951	.2198
	(.46)	(.09)	(.29)	(.59)
Constant	-.9879	-5.678	-3.716	-2.417
	(-.27)	(-1.26)	(-1.14)	(-.69)
Foreign	--	--	--	-.8938
				(-.57)
Summary Statistics				
Pseudo R-square	0.554	0.574	0.515	0.571
Chi-square	82.94	85.94	76.46	85.78

T-statistics in parentheses, * indicates significance at the 10 percent level and ** indicates a five percent level

The second column replaces OVERLAP with OVERLAPA, the variable that measures the maximum possible overlap. As noted above, this variable (OVERLAPA) is subject to potential bias, in that it is an index based on judgements made after the firm's decisions are known. On the other hand, given multiple products made in the same factory, it may be possible to craft innovative settlements that involve selling know-how and equipment to a related firm without selling production facilities. Thus, the use of either overlap variable runs some potential risk. The table shows, however, that the choice of overlap variables has no material effect on the results.

A third test considers a different efficiency variable. The average length of the staff memos varies over the period, and therefore a simple page count may fail to appropriately proxy efficiencies. Although the use of the log formulation and the time trend may minimize this problem, column three considers an efficiency page count normalized by the total number of pages in the BC and BE memos. Thus, the efficiency variable becomes the ratio of the pages on efficiencies to total pages. Again a log specification is used. The results are still very similar, with the efficiency effect in the settle equation falling somewhat in significance.

The final equation examines whether the foreign ownership of the acquiring firm affects its choice of fight, fold or settle. As shown in column 4, no effect was found. Thus, we do not have reason to believe that foreign firms behave differently in these circumstances than their domestic counterparts.

In conclusion, Table 4 shows that the results in Table 3 are remarkably robust. We can conclude that the size of the overlap affects decisions, with firms involved in deals with small overlaps almost certain to settle and firms involved in deals with large overlaps more likely to fight. Efficiencies are also important. If efficiencies are relatively large, the firm is more likely to fight to save the proposed merger. Settlements are also affected by efficiencies, with firms tending to abandon, rather than settle, transactions with larger efficiencies. The merits of a case appear to play

24

a role in the litigation decision. The significance of the Herfindahl interaction variable implies that firms believe that entry barriers are a necessary condition for a merger to be blocked in court. This result is compatible with the recent developments in merger law that have raised the importance of barriers to entry (see Kleit and Coate, Forthcoming). Moreover, the significance of the Herfindahl-barrier/collusion variable (HERFC) offers some evidence for the proposition that courts also require an explanation of how collusion will lead to a competitive problem in the moderate ranges of the Herfindahl index. The value of the transaction also plays a role in the decision, with large deals more likely to end in litigation.

B. Application of the Model: Predictions vs. Actual Outcomes

To apply the model, it is useful to show that it predicts the various types of outcomes reasonably well. The simplest approach is to examine how the model (from column 1 of Table 3) predicts given data which should be suggestive of a particular outcome. For a case that has attributes equal to the sample mean of those cases that folded, the model predicts a 90 percent chance of folding, with a 4 percent chance of a settlement and a 6 percent chance of litigation. For a case with attributes equal to the sample mean of those cases where the firms chose to settle, settling has a 91 percent chance of occurring, while folding is expected to occur with a 9 percent likelihood. Finally, for a case where the attributes are equal to that of the sample mean for the cases that ended in litigation, fighting is expected to occur with a 73 percent probability. Folding is the primary other alternative with almost a 27 percent chance. These results suggest that the model performs relatively well for average cases.

Table 5 examines how well the model (again, column one of Table 3) predicted the actual outcome of the merger cases. Fitted values were computed for each data point and the result with the largest probability (in each case over 50 percent) is assumed to be the predicted outcome. The model predicts correctly 54 percent the cases that end in litigation correctly. The model is much more accurate with settlements with a success rate of over 90 percent. Finally, the model identifies 80 percent of the abandoned mergers. Overall, the model predicts 81 percent of the cases correctly.

Of the 14 cases where the model did not predict the actual outcome, four cases (two of which were fights) had actual outcomes with probabilities over 40 percent. In two cases, the third highest probability represented the actual choice. The first involved an innovative settlement (as discussed in section III-A) and the second involved a case that ended in litigation under unusual circumstances. In the eight remaining cases, three were situations where the parties chose fighting (predicted probabilities 31 percent, 23 percent and 21 percent) over folding (69 percent, 77 percent and 78 percent), two were cases where folding (26 percent and 24 percent) were chosen over settling (74 percent and 75 percent), two involved folding (36 percent and 34 percent) over fighting (63 percent and 66 percent) and in one case the parties decided to settle (22 percent) instead of fold (77 percent). Based on these results, it appears that the model generally eliminates one of the choices.

Table 5

Prediction Table for Historical Data

Predicted Outcome

		Fight	Fold	Settle	Total	% Correct
	Fight	7	6	0	13	54
Actual Outcome	Fold	3	24	3	30	80
	Settle	0	2	27	29	90
	Total	10	32	30	72	81

C. Applications of the Model: Sensitivity

Some indication of the impacts of particular variables can be gained by reviewing what effects they have on the probability of each outcome, given our basic model of Table 3, column 1. For example, assuming a case has the attributes described by the mean of the total sample, Table 6 shows that firms will fold with a 70.4 percent probability, settle with a 24.5 percent probability, and fight with only a 5.1 percent probability. Holding all other variables constant and raising the overlap variable one standard deviation to 85.5 percent generates an 4.0 percent increase in the probability of folding to 74.4 percent, a 22.9 percent decrease in the settle rate to a minuscule 1.6 percent, and a 18.9 percent rise in the fight probability to 24.0 percent. Similarly, holding all other variables constant and reducing the overlap variable one standard deviation to 10.5 percent reduces the fold probability 47.5 percent to 22.9 percent, raises the settle rate 52.2 percent to 76.7 percent, and lowers the fight rate 4.7 percent to an unlikely 0.4 percent.

Table 6
Sensitivity Analysis of Base Model

Scenario	Probability of Folding	Probability of Settling	Probability of Fighting
Sample Means	0.7041	0.2449	0.0510
Raising OVERLAP 1 s.d	0.7444	0.0157	0.2399
Lowering OVERLAP 1 s.d.	0.2294	0.7669	0.0037
Raising Effic. 1 s.d	0.6659	0.0739	0.2602
Lowering Effic. 1 s.d.	0.4753	0.5183	0.0064
Raising HERFB 1 s.d	0.7229	0.2569	0.0153
Lowering HERFB 1.13 s.d.	0.6068	0.2075	0.1858

Standard deviation is denoted s.d.
Predictions generated using model of Table 3, column 1.

Changing the level of efficiencies has similar, if smaller effects. Raising the efficiency variable one standard deviation while holding all other variables at their sample means generates a reduction in the fold rate to 66.6 percent, a decrease in the settle rate to 7.4 percent, and an increase in the fight rate to 26.0 percent. Lowering the efficiency variable one standard deviation reduces the probability of folding from the base case of 22.9 percent to 47.5 percent, raises the settle rate to 51.8 percent, and lowers the fight rate to a tiny 0.6 percent.

Raising the structure variable HERFB one standard deviation while holding all other variables at their sample means has little effect on outcomes, raising the probability of folding 1.9 percent, the probability of settling 1.2 percent, while reducing the chances of fighting 3.6 percent. Lowering the HERFB variable 1.13 standard deviations (to 0, representing a case with no barriers to entry perceived by BE staff), however, has a somewhat larger impact. In this scenario, the probability of folding falls 9.7 percent to 60.7 percent, the probability of settling declines 3.8 percent to 20.8 percent, while the probability of fighting rises 13.5 percent to 18.6 percent.

One can also apply the model to proposed mergers to predict the likely response to a Commission merger challenge. Through the end of fiscal 1992, the Commission challenged four proposed horizontal transactions. All of these cases ended in settlements, with the parties selling off offending assets or technology. In three of these cases, the model predicted a probability of settlement of more than 90 percent, while in the fourth the settlement probability exceeded 70 percent. Thus, for fiscal year 1992, the model has been very successful in predicting the outcomes of FTC merger cases.

V. CONCLUSION

The results of the fight, fold or settle model have clear implications for antitrust policy. The econometric model shows that firms are very unlikely to litigate when the overlap is small, the value of the transaction is low and/or the acquiring firm is large. These conditions encompass a wide range of FTC cases. Thus, the FTC (and likely its sister agency, the Department of Justice) must be seen in large part as regulators, not law enforcers, because there is no viable independent external review of a large number of their bureaucratic decisions. To retain a judicial standard in antitrust cases, the decision makers must therefore act as courts and assign the litigation staff the burden of proof when making enforcement decisions.

The model also sheds light on the firm's decision-making process. The significance of the efficiency variable appears to suggest that some mergers are efficiency motivated, because firms are more willing to incur litigation costs to complete a transaction when efficiencies are high. Similarly, firms appear less willing to enter into settlements in markets where significant efficiencies are likely to be available. Firms appear to base their litigation decisions on the merits of a merger case as interpreted by the case law. We found evidence that firms' decisions were influenced by the existance of barriers to entry in addition to the size of the relevant Herfindahl index. Thus, attorneys and consultants can use information on efficiencies and market structure to predict the likelihood of litigation and settlement.

BIBLIOGRAPHY

Coate, Malcolm B. "Economics, the Guidelines and the Evolution of Merger Policy," Antitrust Bulletin 37(4) (Winter 1992); The Journal of Reprints for Antitrust Law and Economics 21 (2) (1992): 927-954.

Coate, Malcolm B., Richard S. Higgins and Fred S. McChesney, "Bureaucracy and Politics in FTC Merger Challenges," Journal of Law and Economics 33(2) (October 1990) 463-482.

Coate, Malcolm, B. and Fred McChesney, "Empirical Evidence on FTC Enforcement of the Merger Guidelines," Economic Inquiry 30(2) (April 1992) 277-293.

Comanor, William S., and Lawrence J. White, "Market Power or Efficiency: A Review of Antitrust Standards," Review of Industrial Organization 7(2) (1992) 105-116.

Fershtman, Chaim and Kenneth L. Judd, "Equilibrium Incentives in Oligopoly," American Economic Review 77:5 (December 1987) 927-940.

Ginsburg, Douglas H., "Antitrust as Antimonopoly," Regulation 14(3) (Summer 1991) 91-100.

Hausman, Jerry and Daniel McFadden, "Specification Test for the Multinomial Logit Model," Econometrica 52(5) (September 1984) 1219-1240.

Johnson, Ronald and Allen Parkman, "Premerger Notification and the Incentive to Merge and Litigate," Journal of Law, Economics & Organization, 7(1) (1991) 145-162.

Joskow, Paul L., "The Role of Transaction Cost Economics in Antitrust and Public Utility Regulatory Policies," Journal of Law, Economics, & Organization 7(Special Edition) (1991) 53-83.

Khemani, R. S. and D. M. Shapiro, "An Empirical Analysis of Canadian Merger Policy," Journal of Industrial Economics , forthcoming.

Kleit, Andrew N. and Malcolm B. Coate, "Are Judges Leading Economic Theory? Sunk Costs, the Threat of Entry and the Competitive Process," Southern Economic Journal (forthcoming).

Kolasky, William J., Jr., Phillip A. Proger, and Roy T. Englert, "Antitcompetitive Mergers: Prevention and Cure," pages 49-84 in Franklin M. Fisher, ed., Antitrust and Regulation, MIT Press (1985) Cambridge, MA.

Landes, William M., "An Economic Analysis of the Courts," Journal of Law and Economics 14(1) (April 1971) 61-108.

Lopatka, John E., and James Mongoven, "After Preliminary Relief in Merger Cases is Denied, What Then?", mimeo, University of South Carolina Law School, (1992).

Maddala, G.S., Limited-dependent Qualitative Variables In Econometrics, Cambridge University Press (1986) New York.

McCubbins, Matthew D., Roger G. Noll, and Barry R. Weingast, "Administrative Procedures as Instruments of Political Control," Journal of Law, Economics, and Organization, 3(2) (Fall 1987) 243-77.

Milgrom, Paul, and John Roberts, "Predation, Reputation, and Entry Deterrence," Journal of Economic Theory, 27(2) (1982) 280-312.

Perloff, Jeffrey M. and Daniel L. Rubinfeld, "Settlements in Private Antitrust Litigation," in Private Antitrust Litigation: New Evidence, New Learning edited by Lawrence White (Cambridge, Mass.: MIT Press, 1988).

Posner, Richard A., "The Behavior of Administrative Agencies," Journal of Legal Studies 1(2) (June 1972) 305-347.

U.S. Department of Justice, "Department of Justice and Federal Trade Commission Horizontal Merger Guidelines," Antitrust Trade and Regulation Report, No. 1559, (April 2, 1992)

www.ingramcontent.com/pod-product-compliance
Lightning Source LLC
Chambersburg PA
CBHW081316180526
45170CB00007B/2734